WOMEN ARE AHEAD OF THE GAME

BEWARE OF WHO YOU TRY TO PLAY ON

Based on a true story by

B Hatten

iUniverse, Inc.
New York   Bloomington

Women Are Ahead of the Game

Beware of who you try to play on

iUniverse books may be ordered through booksellers or by contacting:

iUniverse
1663 Liberty Drive
Bloomington, IN 47403
www.iuniverse.com
1-800-Authors (1-800-288-4677)

ISBN: 978-1-4401-0607-1 (pbk)
ISBN: 978-1-4401-0608-8 (ebk)

Printed in the United States of America

iUniverse rev. date: 12/09/08

Acknowledgments

I would like to specifically highlight and applaud my sister and my wife, who was directly instrumental and encouraging to me to write this book. However, both wish to remain anonymous. I can't mention their names. This book is a true story and is a noble mission to educate men and women in the world we live in today about the evils of cheating in a relationship or marriage. Both men and women are full of greed and deception to satisfy their own cravings, never taking their mates feelings into consideration. However, men and women should never judge a book by its cover, and realize that all players always end up by themselves. Some men and women today are full of ignorance, when it comes to love and money. There is always a price to pay for lust. Remember, true love shouldn't cost a thing. Real love is priceless.

INTRODUCTION

This book is about how people use and play with people's emotions. Everyone knows the word love is suppose to be beautiful, not painful. Sometimes we as human beings forget what real love is all about, and we also sometimes want our cake and eat it too. The word love always gets people in trouble, when you know you don't really mean it, but when it's family, the old saying is, never mess with family. Let's get this journey started.

DISCLAIMER

There are a lot of people in the world we live in, going through problems in there relationships. Some people face the truth and work through there problems, but there are some people that just don't care about there relationships, or hurt feelings from there mate. These people often keep living a lie, when you really love someone, you should not cheat on them. Love is suppose to be beautiful, not painful. However, in my own opinion, this true story is to educate human minds that there are consequences behind cheating. Hopefully this book will change the frame of mind, of both men and women, to wake up before it's too late. Sometimes it takes losing the best thing that ever happened, to a man or woman, to see that there are consequences for every unfaithful move that you make. This world we live in today is really just one big soap opera. In my opinion, a woman is smarter than a man, and sooner or later, you will get busted, because a woman is always ahead of the game!

Bernard Hatten

CHAPTER ONE

She was Devoted

I was living down south and decided to move back home after a failed relationship. Suddenly I thought, wow! I am back in New Jersey. I noticed how much things changed, the atmosphere was different, especially people. However, people were mean looking and crazy and looked like they didn't have a care in the world. I was intimidated for a while because I haven't lived here in 20 years. So I stayed to myself. I worked everyday and minded my own business. I was always closest to my little sister Meia. I spoiled her as a little girl. We were always close. I was her big brother. No one mess with her because people knew I'd flip if you messed with her. I watched her grow up and go to college and be successful. However, while in college, she met a guy named Bobby. Meia always spoke highly of Bobby. Sometimes I thought too highly because after meeting and talking with Bobby, well I thought he was nice. But I always felt he could have been

1

an undercover faggot, because of the way Bobby talked. He had a very soft voice! And to me he didn't have enough bass in his voice. That always bothered me, it made me wonder was he a man or a mouse. However, Bobby was always quiet. Everyone knows the quiet ones you have to watch. Bobby seemed to be a very nice gentleman. He was always helpful and he got along with the family, but Bobby had a lot of baggage from a previous marriage. I always wondered why he had gotten divorced. I asked, he never had given me a straight answer, the subject was always changed. So I let it go, never really saying anything else about it, but I knew something was wrong, because Bobby was too quiet. He had skeletons in his closet. It always made me wonder if he had been with men and didn't want to talk about it. So as time went by, I discovered that if a man's too quiet, something's wrong, like I said before, because I am a man myself, that's when you know we are hiding something. Watch out ladies, your man is up to something. I've seen Bobby get cell phone calls and walk away from me, while talking to the person on the phone, then see the strange look in his eyes. Then I replied, "Who was that?", then he say, "Oh just someone from work", or it was his kids' babysitter. I heard the womans' voice: He didn't have to lie to me. Bobby was very manipulative, if he didn't get his way. He'd catch an attitude with my sister, then say she wasn't acting mature. He'd reply, "Your still young". Bobby was 15 years older than Meia. He thought he could control her mind as well as her body, because he felt he was older and more mature. Sometimes I just looked on, because as long as Bobby wasn't putting his hands on Meia, everything was fine. He never put his hands on Meia, because Bobby was beating her with mind games. I continued to watch him. Bobby could never look me in the eye. I wondered about that. What was really going on in Bobbys' head? Some guys think because their older, their smarter. They think that their always one step ahead of a woman. A lot of men should know what I've known and was taught, a woman thinks in her sleep. When we are lying in bed snoring, a woman is thinking. Now that I was taught at age 16. Women are taking over the business world, especially large companies. They say women have more powerful minds. I've always wondered why men try to outsmart women, you can't! That's the bottom line. You will get busted in the long run, if you have cheating and lying ways! Meia never looked at another man because Bobby had her nose wide open and she treated him like a king.

CHAPTER 2

Meia is Always Happy

I always watched Meias' attitude. She was a god fearing woman. Meia went to church every Sunday. I never saw my sister do anything wrong. Meia didn't even curse. I was thinking out loud, Bobby was a lucky man, because the average woman would curse your ears off, especially if you have done something that they didn't approve of. Then Meia would come home from church in a very good mood. She would cook a beautiful meal for us and she would sing around the house. That was when I knew someone was very happy. I had never really seen Meia this happy. I was thinking to myself, damn this guy is good. I love to see Meia happy, because when she is happy, Meia is a great cook. Everyone knows that the way to a mans' heart is through his stomach, that goes for any man. I was also taught that as a little kid coming up in the south. However, having southern roots pretty much made me suspicious of guys. Because a lot of them just want one thing and that's sex. Now a days people have sex with no feelings behind it, again the bottom line is, I just didn't want anyone messing over my sister, because she was my baby sister and I didn't play games when it came to her! Men now are different and don't care about who they bang and mess over. Years ago, the average guy use to care about who's sister that is, or who's mother that is. Now, bang bang move on to the next one. I've always sat down and talked to my sister, telling her the real difference between a chickenhead and a prostitute. There both the same. A real woman is self sufficient and do things herself, and not ask a man for anything. That shows character and knowing you didn't have to sleep with a guy for money to get your hair or nails done. Now that's a classy woman, who has pride in herself. These were the type of women Bobby was use to going out with, women with no class! We as men, sometimes forget where we come from. We were raised with classy mothers and fathers, most of us anyway that has morals and values. Most women today don't understand the word shame. A lot of women think they can do what a man can do. I'd say yes in the working and professional world, but if a man walks down the street with his penis out, 10 years from now people will forget that. But if a woman does it and she's also known for sleeping around, she is then called a whore! All what I'm replying is, women have to make better choices before they let their heart run wild and free, because after a bitter breakup, some women never recover, and that man leaves a bad taste in their mouths'. This is how a cycle gets started in women having trust issues. Some women turn to other women, this starts the gay cycle, in some cases. In other cases, women lock their hearts into a deep hard shell, and makes it very hard for the next man, all because the man she use to have was a jerk. One bad apple sometimes spoils the whole bunch in some womens' eyes, especially after a very bad experience. However, this is self explanatory, this is what I've always thought about Bobby, he was a smooth operator. I was always taught from a young teenager, that there's always someone smoother than you. As you keep reading this book, your going to find out who was the smoothest one!

CHAPTER 3

Bobby Acting Strange

I always told my sister Meia that if you feel in your gut that somethings wrong, go with your first instinct, because your heart never lies. Meia felt something was wrong with Bobby, he wasn't acting right. She caught Bobby in a couple of lies, and then Meia started to think, somethings not right. Bobby would come home from work with an attitude, and many of times wouldn't look her straight in the face. He would always talk to her, but not looking at her face. Well, Meia called me one night, explaining the situation. I told her, maybe he was having a rough day at work, that's still not a good reason to mistreat your woman. That's how a lot of relationships are broken up, because of lack of communication, not even trying to talk about what is bothering you. Being a man, I know the feeling. We'd rather keep the problem all bottled up inside, that makes the situation worse, not talking about it. Normally when a man has attitudes, he's mainly in deep thought. Sometimes we are selfish, because we think our problem is our problem. But when someone really loves you, they care about what your thoughts are, because when you hurt, if it's true love between you and your mate, they're hurting to, that's a two way street. However, it's not a good idea to hide anything from the person you love. You should talk about it out in the open, don't hold it inside, this was Bobbys' problem. He never liked to talk about anything to Meia, that's not a healthy way of living. People die everyday from stress and heart attacks, because they never talk about what's on their mind and keep it bottled up. But somehow, I always thought after meeting and getting to know Bobby, he was selfish and insecure. I told Meia something was wrong, because when a man starts acting funny, it's normally someone else. Meia replied, "He's not like that, I don't think". Meia always went out of her way to keep this man satisfied. Meia did everything for this man. Sometimes I thought Bobby was unappreciative of the things Meia did for him. Meia would come home after a hard days' work, and then go to Bobbys' house and cook and clean for him. All the men I know, including myself, would kill for a woman like that. Some of the women I dated, didn't cook or clean. When it came to cooking, she'd grab the telephone and call the fast Lucky Chinese Restaurant. I am from the south, and there's nothing like a good home cooked meal. When I first start dating a woman, one of the first questions I'd always ask is, "Do you cook?". Bottom line is, Bobby was being treated like royalty, and I couldn't understand why he was mistreating my sister. I was thinking to myself, that it could only be another woman was starting to get in Bobbys' ear. Well, I am a man and I know these things. This is normally the case when a man sees something else he wants to stick his teeth into, and a man will use every resource to try and breakup with the other woman, or just play both of them at one time. This is pretty common in todays society with men and women. The tides have turned years ago. Men were more prominent to do this to women, but now they average about the same. In the long run, men and women hurt themselves by living double lives, and often forget the truth, and forget who they already have at home, that's logic in its' self, being faithful and true. Being dishonest in a relationship almost always gets you in trouble. Bobby really didn't seem like that type, but I was thinking that he was a smooth operator. I always believed that he just told women what they wanted to hear. I did notice that Bobby always tried to live beyond his means, that's the problem most men have. We want the big car, and the big house on the hill, and really can't afford them. Some guys like to live this way, by showing women the materialistic things in life. In some cases it's really a fraud, because a lot of guys have fancy cars and have nowhere to sleep. A lot of guys sleep at different womens' houses or they sleep in their cars, I've seen it. Women have to stop and think for a minute, if a guy always takes you to a motel instead of his house, or makes excuses about where he lives, that should be a red light. A real man will tell you the truth about where he lives and his problems. Sometimes us men make excuses, because of the fear of embarrassment and rejection. I've always thought that if a woman couldn't accept you as you are, then she's not the one for you. This is my point, Bobby didn't lie about his past marriage or his kids, he stayed truthful and honest about that situation, that went a long way with me, because some men don't own up to their responsibility and keep it secret. There are some men that continue their path of lies, by living a double life, and playing more than one woman at a time. That's why some men are not stable, because they want to play the field, and never having a commitment. Some men are married and still play the field. I think men sometimes forget, when they got married, they took an oath and promise to love and cherish their bride for the rest of their lives, but we as men let other thoughts roam through our minds, especially looking at other women, and fantasizing about the idea of cheating, and we lust after beauty, mainly tits and fat asses, just putting the truth out, this is fact and not fictional. The truth hurts, because we think with our small head and not with the big one, that's what gets most men in trouble every time, because of the small head thinking. I had a feeling that this was Bobbys' problem, when your in a commitment, which means love, you can't be lusting after other women, but me coming from a two parent household it was hard, because I saw it all. Being a man, we think that we are smooth, by lying to our woman, being very deceptive and having extra affairs on the side. I seen this in my own immediate family. A lot of times this gets the man in trouble, because that's when other problems come into play, like having children from different women and hiding it, well at least trying to hide it. When I was a kid, my grandmother always told, me, what you do in the dark will soon come to light, and that's so true, because later in life, I found out that I had other sisters and brothers. All from a man living a double life, never honoring his commitment to his marriage, and lived a lie for 30 years by not telling his wife the truth, but it came to light, because it ate him up inside. It didn't really come to light until I came home. When I was a kid, there were roomers that he was seen with other women, and my sister looked like a twin to my half sister, so there was no denying the situation. We also heard that they lived around the corner from us, and went to the same school that we attended. Now we know the facts, the roomer was true. All what I'm saying is, if you hear a roomer concerning your lover, investigate it. Sometimes it might hurt you to find out the truth, but it's better to find out now, than later, so you can move on with your life. Some people can't move on, because of the fear of being by themselves. Sometimes people are happier being by themselves, until they find someone that really makes them happy, and there not going to cheat on them, and just keep it real!

CHAPTER 4

False Excuses for Working Late

However, there are some guys that lay guilt trips. Most of the time, guilt is exercized when men know they are cheating. We start arguments that form into big ones over nothing, because our subconscious is eating at us. Men often use the excuse of an argument to stay out late, and among other things. We often feel that a big argument is the key to lay the big guilt trip. Most men use this tactic, and being a man, I know that, because I've done it in my past, then going to see the other woman. That is what we do as men to make cheating feel alright, but it's not alright. Cheating in a relationship is a disaster. It's wrong, disrespectful, distrustful, and most of all dishonest. This goes for women too. There are some women out there, that are just like men. They flirt and also, bring trouble to the household. A woman can also hide things, as well as a man, but a woman will sometimes admit her guilt before a man does, because her conscious would be killing her. Although a man, speaking from personal experience, he will lie to the end, until he gets caught. I never thought Bobby was that type of person, because he was so quiet, and always under my sister, watching her every move, even if she went to the grocery store, Bobby was there. No one would ever suspect anything like this from Bobby. There's a lot of men in this world, that are just like Bobby. They will smile in your face, and all the time, trying to find someone to take your place, because some men are not satisfied with one woman. There is a new trend of women in this world. These women don't bother to look for a ring, or ask a man if he's married, or involved with someone. These women don't care. They look at what a fine ride your driving, how fat your wallet is, and how much you make in a week. This is sad and repulsive, because this cycle goes on. A lot of men and women wonder why there not married, maybe because they've slept with everybody, no one wants sloppy seconds, or a person that's laid more than carpet. Personally speaking, I wouldn't want a woman that I couldn't go in the grocery store with, because of fear of her running into someone she had slept with. A real woman should be able to count how many men she has slept with on two hands, that's what I look for during conversation, I am blunt and straight to the point. I am not trying to marry or date a hooker. Some women today have a price and will do anything for money. A good woman is hard to find and real love shouldn't cost anything. Meia was a good woman. She had real love in her heart for this man. Why is Bobby treating her this way?, I often thought, but pretty soon, whatever Bobby is doing, it will come out sooner or later. I was always taught to never mess with a god fearing Christian woman, because the truth always prevail, it comes to the light. However, Meia is a smart woman and well educated, like I replied earlier in the book. Meia graduated with honors in high school and was the valedictorian. Meia was the smartest young lady in the whole school. I don't know why Bobby is acting funny with Meia. When we were kids, I could never put one over on Meia, she was always one step ahead of the game. I feel sorry for Bobby if he's cheating on Meia, because you can never get one over on Meia.

CHAPTER 5

A strange Woman Calling the House

Every woman has a golden rule about female incoming calls in a relationship, if it's not your mother or sister, hang the phone up. Some, or most guys, don't understand that. A lot of men have male egos in their own house. Most men figure that if they're paying the bills in the household, no one can tell them what to do. I always felt that Bobby had this type of attitude and behavior, because of his demeanor, and I always felt that this type of behavior had a hand in ending Bobbys' marriage, because Bobby was not being honest to his wife. Bobby was thinking, if it's not my way, it's the highway. A lot of men feel this way, because they think their the head of the household, and they can do anything they want, but in fact, there are more women who are the head of the household, and their husband respects them. There are some men who are not going for that, some men think that they are more superior than women. There are men who fear women, because of their professionalism, and don't think a woman should be the head of anything, but riding the top of their little head. This is just some of the perceptions that some men think. I think that's not being fair to a woman, or to a relationship. I think that's what Bobbys' perception of a woman was, and not giving a woman her full respect. However, Meia called me on a Saturday replying, "Someone keeps calling the house and hanging up". I replied to her, "Did anyone say anything?". Meia replied, "No, whoever was on the other end of the line, just heard my voice and hung up". I replied, "Maybe it was a bill collector". Meia replied, No, because a bill collector would leave a message". I started thinking out loud, but didn't want to give my sister the bad thoughts I was thinking, because I was once in a bad relationship, and some of the same signs were there. I asked my sister, "Meia, do you want my honest opinion?". She replied, "Yes". I am seven years older than Meia, and she likes to hear my advice on what I think about the situation. Meia didn't like to hear bad news of any kind, but I had to give it to Meia straight, no holds barred. Meia knew I was older and had more experience in relationships then she had, so I told Meia about one relationship I was in for Meia to get my point. I was living with a woman for ten years, and never thought she would lie to me or cheat on me, but this woman cheated on me with several men, right under my nose. I was blinded by love, until I got smart, and figured out what's good for the goose, is good for the gander. This woman had my nose wide open and my eyes blinded. This woman was slick as Crisco grease. Once I discovered she was cheating, I didn't say a word, but we would get into arguments, and I was the one who had to take anger management classes. When I felt an argument coming on, I would go outside for a 2 hour time out, all of this for love. The woman I was with didn't really care about me, because if she did care, she wouldn't be cheating on me. One day during the time out, I met a woman. This woman was nice and made me feel special, because she would go out of her way to speak to me, so then, this woman invited me to her house. I was thinking, I can't go, because I am in a relationship, and two wrongs don't make a right. The woman I was with kept starting arguments, so one Friday I was taking a time out, that's when I ran into Sherry, the woman I met during a time out. We talked and exchanged phone numbers. I told her that I was involved with someone, but Sherry didn't care, that's how some women are. I told Sherry that when she wanted to call me, have her son call, that way it doesn't raise suspicion, so we did that for a while. I had finally gave in, and started loving everytime we had gotten into an argument, so I could take a time out, and go to Sherrys' house, and I started seeing Sherry. However, Sherry fell in love with me, and wanted me for herself. I knew this wasn't right, so I slowed the relationship down, because I knew the woman I was already involved with was going to be a problem, because we had broken up before, and this woman didn't give up. She wanted me back at all cost, but I was tired of the time outs, and the flip floppiness of the relationship. Sherry started calling the house and hanging up, not saying anything. She would send her son out, hoping he would see me during my afternoon or evening walks. However, I was explaining this to Meia, but if you want to get the conclusion of that story, you'll have to buy my next book, If My Heart Had Eyes It Would Cry. A woman never expects that it's another woman calling and hanging up on them, this is normally a sign that something is going on. Meia replied to me, "Do you think it's another woman?". I replied to her "Yes", and also replied again, "I hated to tell you that, but I guess you have gotten your answers through my little story", so now Meias' eyes are wide open and full of suspicion. However, the following weekend, a woman called and left a message for Meias' boyfriend Bobby. Meia didn't tell him about the message, so Bobby checked his messages, and Meia asked him, "Who is she?". Bobby replied, "A woman I work with". Meia didn't think about it anymore, until the woman started calling everyday, sometimes interrupting dinner and quiet time. Meia asked Bobby to tell Shirley, the woman who was calling, not to call his house, anymore, because Meia felt that this was disrespectful to her. Meia asked Bobby, "Does she know you have a girlfriend?". Bobby replied, "Yes, but she don't care, she's just a friend from work".

CHAPTER 6

Not Respecting Your Mates Wishes

However, Meia was now upset about being disrespected, and Bobby wasn't really understanding how Meia was feeling, but if you put the shoe on the other foot, Bobby would be mad also, if some man was calling Meia everyday. There is nothing that important to talk about everyday, only if you are cheating on your mate, girlfriend, or boyfriend, etc. People sometimes use excuses and crutches to cheat on their spouse or mate, which is crazy and uncalled for. I was always taught, if you didn't want a person anymore, it's best to tell them and not lead them on, because that hurts feelings and breaks hearts. No one wants a broken heart. Feelings are fragile, like glass, if a glass slips out of your hand, it breaks, so being human, we often slip like that glass in relationships. We often drop the ball and shatter peoples' hearts, by thinking about our own needs, and not caring about no one elses', and never thinking about that there are consequences behind everything we do. Bobby was thinking like a typical man. We always think that we are slick and conning, but in most cases, some men think that they are stunning and can get away with anything. I was always taught that a woman thinks, while a man sleeps. It still shocks me, that men still think that they are smarter than women, but in this case, Bobby thought he was smarter than everyone, because he had a degree in computer science, and he could fix and mend anything, especially a womans' heart. He figured that he always knew what to tell a woman, when things got hot. Bobby thought he was a smooth operator, at least that's what he thought, like I said before. Well personally, I always thought Bobby had girl tendencies, because of the way he talked. I was thinking out loud to myself, this man has some nerve trying to cheat on someone, with his gay looking ass, especially my sister. Like I said, there's nothing like a brothers' love. Every man will be a protector of his sister, and won't let anything happen to them, if they could help the situation. Bobby had some nerve to treat my sister the way he was, having all that baggage, plus kids from another marriage, which ended in divorce, Now I am two seconds from getting involved. No man wants to see his sister crying and sobbing around the house, and not being themselves. I was thinking to myself, I have to do something to help Meia, because she loved Bobby. I was beginning to wonder, if Bobby was putting his hands on her. I asked Meia, she replied to me, "No!", then I replied to Meia, "But you are not yourself, you are normally happy go lucky. I am not going to sit back and let some man take advantage of you", I also told Meia, "Please let me know if you need me for anything, because I really want to kick his ass, but if you say everything is alright, then I believe you". I replied again, "Just let me know". By the way, my name is Calvin, I am Meias' brother. I've always had my sisters' back, even protecting her when she was in grade school. This kind of bond can never be broken. However, we as men sometimes try to play a woman stupid, thinking they'll believe anything, or every word that comes out of our mouths, but women are smart, they keep quiet and observe, before they react or reply to anything. Like I mentioned before, after a man is caught cheating, some women will forgive, but won't forget, and some women will end it, because it shouldn't have happened in the first place. However, there are a lot of men that are stupid, like I replied before, their wives or girlfriends are drop dead gorgeous, but they would rather cheat and sleep with women that are drop dead ugly, because men figure they're easy prey, and will take any penis available, not caring if they are married or unavailable. In my own opinion, those type of women have self esteem problems, because they're willing to put theirselves at risk, for a little dick, not realizing that there hurting a relationship or marriage. This is very common in todays society, which is very shameful, not caring about another human beings feelings, only taking into consideration their own wants and needs. Whatever happened to respect, honor, and dignity? In todays world, there's a lot of men that would sell their soul for a strange piece of ass. Some men don't even pay their own personal bills, they would rather spend the money on some dirty trick or hoe, instead of taking care of their responsibilities. There are some men who are users, these men go around using good women, making it bad for the next one, like I replied before, once a woman has a bad experience, a woman starts thinking that every man's the same, like I said before, one bad apple spoils the whole bunch. We as men need to wake up from this demented mind syndrome that we are having, and start respecting our wives and girlfriends, and stop trying to lie to them. A real man doesn't do this. Your wife shouldn't have to take a back seat to no other woman! Ladies, please remember this, watch the young girls, they will push up on your man faster than you can bat your eyes. Shirley was five years younger than Meia. Bobby and Meia met in college. Meia was substantially younger than Bobby. We as men often like to think back when we were young. A lot of times men don't want to feel their ages, so we will try to push up on the younger women, just to see if we still got it, and most of the time that lands a marriage or relationship in trouble, because we can't accept that we are happy in a committed relationship. Sometimes we feel as men, we shouldn't show all of our emotion toward one person, but we should when you love someone. However, if a man feels he has to cheat, he should end the relationship, and don't keep living a lie, messing up someone elses' life, that goes for men and women. Remember all men love the rewards of hunting, and whenever a man is hunting, he's not happy in the relationship. We as men often use the term phrase, "What she don't know, it won't hurt her", withholding the truth about something. However, men and women tell small lies that soon turns into larger lies. We as human beings will find it more easier to tell the larger lie after we've gotten away with the smaller ones. Ladies and gentlemen, it's very simple, don't lie to your mate. Ladies and gentlemen, remember if you approach your mate about a lie and they still lie, this should be a red light. This more often develops trust issues. A true loving relationship is not based on lies. Today, there's a lot of marriages and serious relationships that are based on a pack of lies, because men and women are afraid to investigate the truth, fear of finding the truth. Meia wasn't afraid to find the truth. Why keep a relationship or marriage if you don't trust someone?

CHAPTER 7

Solving The Puzzle, Who Is She?

O ne afternoon, Meia was over Bobbys' house and the phone rang, again it was another hang up call. When Bobby got home from work, she replied to him, "There was another hang up call". Bobby started having an attitude, so during the argument, the phone rang again. This time the woman Shirley spoke, she replied, "May I speak with Bobby?", so Meia replied, "Who is this?", she replied, "Shirley", so Meia then replied, "I asked you nicely not to call my house anymore". Shirley replied, "Bobby said I could call anytime I wanted to". Immediately, Meia questioned Bobby while Shirley was still on the phone, replying "Did you say she could call here anytime she wanted to?". Bobby replied, "No!", and then said, "But I told Shirley she could call here, only with a work matter". However, Bobby used his job to try and sleep with women, we later found that out, because Bobby was a computer wizard, and could fix any computerized item. He would use this to get invited into other womens' houses, we also later found out, that he promised to fix Shirleys' computer for her. Meia was also thinking, he fixed more than a computer, because Shirley was calling too much and then disrespecting Meia, Bobbys' girlfriend, so then Meia thought to herself, enough of this. Meia packed her bags and came home. She got tired of being disrespected. We as men know that once a woman gets tired of our shit, she's leaving, no its or buts about it. Bobby was so dumb, he still didn't know why Meia left. He thought it was just because a woman was calling the house. Every man knows, if a woman leaves you, it's because she thinks that you cheated on her, or she has another man, that's normally the case. Bobby has to realize, just because that's his house, and he thinks that he's the boss, Bobby has to know that when you invite a woman in your house and life, all those things that you use to do, has to change. The bachelor life is over, because a woman is always going to make changes, it's no longer just himself, now you have to answer to someone. Well, some men don't think that they have to answer to anyone, because they pay the bills, but that's a lie, men have to always respect their mate or spouse. The old saying is, treat others like you want to be treated, but some men just don't get that, because a lot of them were raised without fathers, and don't know how to respect a woman, or anyone else for that matter. Now Bobby is calling the house everyday, trying to make up with Meia, but Meia wasn't really trying to hear what Bobby was trying to say, because Meia always felt that, if a man would lie to her with a straight face, he'll cheat on me. Bobby swore up and down, that nothing ever happened between him and Shirley. He was begging Meia to take him back, so Meia called me, asking me, what should she do. I replied, "Just take some time to sort everything out. Don't rush it". I then replied, "Meia, I am your brother, just take your time please, because I don't want to have to hurt this man. I told you before, I think that somethings not right, just be patient, time will tell, if this man really loves you. Don't rush back to him, because love hurts, and if you do this too fast, you might be setting yourself up for more hurt, because this man is fifteen years older than you. Bobby figures that he could just step all over you, because he has years of experience of being a master super liar. He figures that your young, and he could tell you anything and keep his charade up, without you having any suspicion on what he's doing!". However, Meia was still confused, so Meia called me one night, she replied, "There's something I want you to do for me, before I even think about going back to him full time, staying in his house". Again, Meia replied to me, "I am not going to be anybodys' fool ever again. This man thinks he's smart, but I am going to show him, who's smarter. My mother didn't raise no fools. He thinks that, because he has a house and a nice car, he can put the wool over my head", so then Meia replied to me, "I need your word, would you help me do something, when I call you telling you, I need help?". I replied to my sister, "I'll do anything I can to help you, but I'm hoping it's something to catch the piece of shit".

CHAPTER 8

Lying to the Very End

S o how many of us men, has promised a woman that we are not going to do something again? We have all fell short of keeping our promises, but that's still no reason to keep doing what we promised to stop. However, Bobby was a good liar, he had years of experience, so Meia decided to go back and stay with him. Two weeks passed, and the phone calls started again. Meia went to Bobby again and questioned him, she said, "Shirley is still calling here. I thought you said, that you told her to don't call here again, not even for a job issue. The woman is still calling here, and we got into an argument on the phone. I am a god fearing woman, I had enough, and I told the bitch to don't call here anymore, then Shirley replied, tell your man to stop calling me and coming over my house". Meia replied, "What bitch?", then Shirley replied, "If you were taking care of your business, your man wouldn't be calling me". Meia then hangs up on

Shirley. Meia then approached Bobby about the situation. Meia replied to Bobby, "Did you go over that bitches' house? I am tired of this shit", so then Meia replied to Bobby, "I need to use your phone. I have to call my brother", so Meia called me, she then replied, "Remember that favor I told you I was going to need?", I replied, "Sure, what?", Meia replied, "I'll tell you tomorrow, I can't talk right now, I'll be over tomorrow". I then replied to Meia, "He's right there, huh?", Meia replies, "Yes", I reply, "OK, see ya tomorrow, can't wait". However, Meia came over the next day. She called me on my cell phone to come down to her house, so then Meia replies to me, "You were right. I think he's cheating on me". I replied, "How do you know? Is that woman Shirley still calling the house?", so I told Meia, "Don't jump to conclusions too fast, get the proof". Meia then replied, "Shirley and I got into a heated argument over the phone". I replied to Meia, "Just be cool, whatever he's doing, it will come out". I made Meia feel better, then she left. A couple of months passed, and Meia calls me, replying, "She calls the house pretty regular. I can't stop it. I'm a bigger woman that she is, I just treat her nice. I am a god fearing woman, and I am not going to stoop to her level, but know I can put my plan into action now, and neither one of them would suspect me of anything". I got to thinking to myself, I wonder what Meia is thinking or planning, because whenever a woman starts thinking, normally that means trouble to a man. Revenge is "Oh so sweet", in a womans' eyes, there's nothing like a woman scorned, where a man has crushed her heart. Some women are not to be played on or played with, because women now fight back, with an eye for an eye. However, there are some women that go through psychological problems and can't deal with a relationship being over, but in my own opinion, men and women should be strong, because there are other fish in the sea, if you are patient enough to wait and give yourself time to heal from the broken relationship, there is a brighter day coming. However, there are so many women that stay in relationships, fearing that they can't find anyone else, or can't be by themselves, some even feel that they are used up, and no one else wants them, but there's always someone for somebody. Some men use this terminology and dialogue to keep their mate into the relationship. Some of the most common statements that are made by men are, "I've taken care of you for years. You have nothing. Where are you going to go? I own everything". In some cases, this convinces a person to stay in the relationship, because they feel that they can't win. However, this wasn't the scenario in Meia and Bobbys' relationship, because Bobby was divorced, and Meia was never married and didn't have any children. I was also thinking to myself, how could this man smile in my face, sometimes twice a week, when he would come to visit the family. Bobby had the whole family fooled, accept Meia and me. He would smile in my mothers' face, always putting on the gentleman look. I just had a feeling that Bobby was to good to be true. What I really was thinking, this man is a crock of shit, putting on the good soon to be son-in-law trip. There's a lot of men and women that start a good show, but the facts are finishing the show. We need to realize as human beings, that everyone has a heart, and no one likes to have a broken heart. Meia was a strong woman, and wasn't going to put up with Bobbys' shit anymore. I was also taught as a kid, to catch the fish, you have to put a big enough worm on the hook, and he'll catch himself, and after all from my standpoint and thoughts, from what Meia was telling me, Bobby was a professional master super liar, and all of his lies were soon coming to an end. Ladies, please stop misusing your bodies, especially our young teenage women, because a lot of them really don't understand what true love is. However, in this day and age a lot of younger women are considered used up, because they have slept with a lot of men. Real women are suppose to set an example for the younger ones. This is a problem in todays society, also with men too, not setting examples for younger men or boys, sending out the wrong signals that it's alright to have more than one woman. Remember ladies and gentlemen, you are being watched by younger people.

CHAPTER 9

The Hospital Visit

However, my sister Meia called me the following Saturday and replies, "I am coming over". I then replied, "Is everything OK?". Meia replied, "Yes, remember that favor I was asking of you when the time was right?", I replied, "Yes, oh shit, are you really going to do something to Bobby?". Meia replies, "Yes, now you can really help me, because Bobby and Shirley wouldn't suspect a thing, to much time has passed, and they are still trying to play me stupid". I then replied to Meia, "Are you sure that you want to carry out whatever you got planned?", Meia then replies, "Yes, because last Monday, Bobby wasn't paying attention to me, and when his phone rang, we both picked up at the same time, but I didn't say anything. I just listened to the whole conversation. It was Shirley. She was calling Bobby to let him know that she wouldn't be home this week, because she was admitted in the hospital". Then I replied,

"What for?", Meia replied, "She really didn't say, but she gave Bobby the name of the hospital and what room she was in and the visiting hours", then I replied, "Why would she be telling Bobby, what hospital she's in, because they are messing around Meia, he's cheating on you". Meia replies, "I almost lost it on the phone, but I kept quiet. I was always taught to never let a man know what he's doing, until the time is right. It's best to stay quiet and observe the situation then trust him, because if I would have said something while they were on the phone, then that would give them time to stop it, because now I would be very suspicious of both of them". Now Meia replies, "I have an acting role for you to play now. I won't feel guilty about anything, because since last Monday, I've been listening to every phone conversation that Bobby had, and most of the time it would be Shirley calling. They were very careful on what they said over the phone". Now Meia replies again, "This is what I want you to do. I put my plan together two weeks ago, because Shirley is going to be in the hospital for 4 weeks. I was just waiting for the right time to spring my trap, but your role is very important". I replied again, "Why is this woman in the hospital?". Meia replies, "I found out it's a blood condition", then I replied back to Meia, "Oh hell no, AIDS", so now I am wondering if I should do it or not. I am not trying to catch no disease for nobody, true enough I love my sister Meia, but AIDS is uncurable. I was thinking to myself, I am not fucking with that bitch if she has AIDS, fuck that, but Meia reassured me that it wasn't AIDS, after she listened to a few more phone calls. My sister always has a crazy look in her eyes when she's up to something. Meia replies to me, "There's nothing to worry about. I have everything worked out. All that I want you to do is date this woman for awhile. I need you to change your name and never bring her to our house, because you never know when they might be together and ride past the house. I don't want Bobby and Shirley to put this together". So I agreed to date this woman, to help my sister get payback on Bobby for cheating on her, and lying to her. However, we do know as men, never do a woman wrong, especially right in her face. There's nothing like a woman scorned. She'll be quiet and say nothing, but all the time she's thinking of ways to pay you back, so remember "men", never do your woman wrong, because what makes you laugh, will also make you cry one day. Bobby didn't think this way. He had a mind of his own, like most men, he always thought about himself, and never in a million years would a man think that his woman I on to him, and his devilish ways. A man will never think that a woman is just as slick, or slicker, then we are. So now as this true story goes on, remember I am Meia' brother Calvin, and my being older than Meia, I never thought that Meia could be so smart and crafty, and intelligence beyond her years. My mind was completely blown away on what Meias' plans were. Me being her oldest brother, like I replied before, I was astonished and being schooled and retooled, about a womans' frame of thought. I am now thinking to myself, yes indeed a woman is smarter than a man in so many ways, it's unbelievable. I was really thinking, Meia must be really tired and fed up with Bobbys' mess, so I had two days to prepare for my big acting job. Meia also found out later, that they were keeping Shirley in the hospital for an extra week. Now Meia really wanted me to move fast. I started watching soap operas, to really put the finishing touches on my acting job, and believe me, watching soap operas and being a man, could be quite boring. I needed to be very sophisticated and educated, to even get to first base with Shirley. So finally Meia called me and replied, "Are you ready?", I replied to Meia, "Yes", Meia replies again saying, "Lets roll, wear your good stuff. I will pick you up at 3:00". I then replied to Meia, "you said this woman is a teacher, do you really think that we can pull this off?", then Meia replies, "This teach needs to be retaught some manners and my name is professor Meia". I then laughed and replied, "See you when you get here". Meia picked me up, and while I am entering her car, Meia replies, "That's my brother", because I was suited and booted from head to toe! We arrive at the hospital. Meia gives me money for roses. I replied to Meia, "Wow, you must really hate this bitch. I don't even know this woman and you are buying her roses". So Meia drops me off at the hospital, but before I got out of the car, Meia replies, "I'll be waiting for you in the parking garage, or just call me on my cell phone", I replied, "OK". I purchased the roses and proceeded to the elevator up to Shirleys' hospital room. I stopped before I entered her room, to remove the laughter from my face, to get serious into my acting role, believe me, it was hard to hold back the laughter, because this in my own opinion, was truly hilarious. I entered the hospital room and saw Shirley for the first time, and believe me, I felt like turning around. She looked aweful. I just keep thinking to myself, I am doing this for Meia. So the nurse replies to me, "May I help you sir?", I then replied, "Hi! Shirley". The nurse replies, "Do you know this man?", I hurried and replied, "My name is John, We met on the train, while traveling to work. I am the bald headed guy that always said good morning to you, and a few times we conversated". Shirley then replies, cutting me off saying, "Oh yes, I remember you". I then replied,

"These roses are for you", then I really, really wanted to bust out laughing something terrible, but held it in. The nurse left us alone, so me and Shirley talked for about 20 minutes. I asked Shirley for her room phone number, and she gave it to me. I started calling Shirley on a daily basis, and may I remind you, this woman didn't know me from a can of paint, and was talking to me on a daily basis, and telling me all her personal business and where she lived. This woman had to be hard up or stupid. My sister Meia would call me everyday from her job, to get daily reports about what we talked about on the phone. Meia was laughing hysterically. Meia wanted all the dirt on her boyfriend Bobby, because when a woman thinks her man is cheating, she'll do anything to find out every little dirty detail. I had to report to Meia like an FBI agent. However, when Shirley got out of the hospital, she wanted to go out on a date with me. I told Meia about it, and I also replied to Meia, "I am already seeing someone and don't have the extra money for a date with a woman, that I don't really like". Meia replied, "I'll pay for everything", I replied, "Wow, you must really hate this bitch", and laughed. I was starting to feel guilty, because Meias' plan was working to perfection, by taking Shirleys' mind off her man. Shirley wasn't the best looking woman, especially when I had seen her in the hospital. Shirley really looked beat. Her hair looked like chickens had a boxing match in it, and her teeth, because of her sickness, looked to be gray and orange. When I saw her teeth, that was a huge turn off, because all that I could think of was that maybe she gave the doctor some head. I never seen teeth like that, but Shirley had a nice personality, maybe that's what Bobby saw in her. Me and Shirley went out on our first date. I had her meet me at a nearby gas station, because I didn't want her to know where I stayed. Shirley didn't even have a telephone number for me, but I had her number. How stupid can Shirley be? How could she date a man and not have a telephone number for him? I began to realize, that this woman wasn't too smart and Shirley was a school teacher. I believe Shirley was desperate for any man. However, when Shirley got dressed up, she really wasn't that bad looking, so during our date, Shirley asked a lot of questions. I gave her all false answers, especially when it came to my true identity. Remember my real name is Calvin, but I told Shirley that my name is John, and not once did this woman ask me if I was going to catch the train in the morning. Remember that was my starting role line with her in the hospital. Me and Shirley had a nice time on our date. We ate at a Chinese restaurant. Shirley really enjoyed that. After the date was over, Shirley was ready to drop me off, and she replied "I can drop you off at home, really it's no problem". I replied, "No!, I live in a bad gang infested neighborhood. I don't want anyone to car-jack you. We will just meet here when I call you". Shirley replied, "OK", but I knew sooner or later, Shirley would start asking a lot of questions. A real woman always does. After I got home, I called Meia and replied, "I think she's getting just a little suspicious. I need to get another cell phone, so that your plan doesn't blow up in your face. This was so Shirley could call me and everything would continue to run smoothly", so Meia agreed. We got another cell phone, just so Shirley could call me. However, our next date was pretty eventful. Shirley forgot her glasses at home. Shirley was driving us to the movies in Jersey City. I have never experienced anything like I did that night. Shirley was side swiping bridges and guard rails. I was crouching in the front seat of her car. There were two lanes of open road, and this woman was hitting the sides of bridges and guard rails. It felt like I was in the car with a blind person. I was scared to death, so when I got home, I called Meia and replied, "That crazy non driving woman almost killed me. I saw my life flash before my eyes". I replied to Meia again, "I don't know if I want to go on another date with this woman. I'd have a better time with a seeing eye dog". So Meia replied, "Was it really that bad?", I then replied, "Trust me, I am an man and Shirley had me hollering like a little bitch. I was yelling, Jesus Christ you're going the wrong way, having my legs up in the air crouching for the impact. My eye balls were as wide as silver dollars". So Meia calmed me down, reassuring me that she was going to finish her plan very soon, so I agreed to continue to help Meia. Shirley was now head over hills for me. Shirleys' attention is now just on me. Now Shirley is real comfortable about discussing her past intimate relationships. She's now telling me what I wanted to hear, so I asked Shirley about her exboyfriend. She replied, "Well, we were friends with benefits. He took me out a few times and he fixed my computer", then I replied, "Are you guys still talking, because I don't want to come in the middle of a relationship". She replied, "No! you are not. I am starting to see that Bobby's a liar", so I replied, "Who's Bobby?" Shirley then replied, "A guy that I met on the train", then I replied, "What happened?". Shirley replied, "Bobby had a woman and didn't tell me, but he swears that she's not his woman. She's just a friend, and he also told me that, I could call his house anytime I wanted to, but some woman named Meia was trying to block my flow, then we had an argument". Then I replied, "Oh really", I paused a minute, then asked Shirley if I could use her bathroom. I was at Shirleys' house, because she couldn't drive and I feared for my life whenever we traveled places, so I planned it where Shirley could pick me up in the daylight on weekends. While in the bathroom, I called my sister Meia on my cell phone. While talking on the phone, I turned on the faucet and opened the bathroom window, so that Shirley couldn't hear me. Remember I had to report everything to Meia, so I told Meia on the phone, "Yes he is seeing her, that's all she replied". Meia then replies, "See if they had sex", I replied, "OK". Meia replied again, "I knew he was fooling around with her", so Shirley started making a lot of noise outside the door, I told Meia that I had to go and that I'll see her when I get home. I left the bathroom and joined Shirley in her living room, then the phone rang. It was Bobby calling, to ask Shirley what was she doing. She replied, "Sitting on the couch with my friend", than an argument insued. I heard Bobby shouting at her through the phone, and Shirley was shouting back, replying to Bobby, "Don't try to tell me how to run my house. You have someone and now I do too". Shirley had already told Bobby that she was seeing a guy named John. Bobby was mad and jealous, and had already threatened me through Shirley, telling me he was going to fuck me up, if he ever saw me. So I returned home and told Meia, that he called her house and argued with her, once she told him that she had company. Meia replied, "That dirty bastard. Now do you see what I was talking about? He deserves everything he gets". I then replied, "Yes, Bobby wanted his cake and eat it too". I didn't like it, not one bit, no one fucks over my sister. His threats gave me power to follow thru with Meias' plan. The following weekend, Shirley wanted me to come over, so she could cook me dinner. I told her yes, again Shirley picked me up at the service station. We went to her house again. She cooked a nice dinner. We were laying on her bed when the phone rang. It was Bobby again, asking her if he could come over. At the same time, while Shirley was on the phone, I had her titty in my mouth, sucking her nipples. Shirley kept telling Bobby "no", then Shirley just hung up on him. I had my cell phone on vibrate, then my phone went off vibrating. I saw the number, it was my sister. I then told Shirley that I had to go to the bathroom, to freshin up before sex. I called my sister back and replied, "This better be good, because I'm headed for home base". Meia replied, "Sex already?", I replied, "Yep!". Meia then replied, "That whore! She must have been really hard up for any man. Most women would have waited at least three or four months before giving up her pussy. That shows you just how some women are in todays society, and really that's nasty. That's why there are so many diseases out here today". I replied again, cutting Meia off saying, "Bobby called her again today". Meia replied, "I knew something was up with Bobby, because he replied to me that he was very tired and had a stressful day at work. He replied to me also, that he had some personal things to do, hoping I would get the hint and go home to my place, so he could sneak and be with Shirley. Huh, but we got that covered, ha!, ha!", Meia was laughing hysterically. Then I replied to Meia again, "You don't have to worry about that, because I'm getting that ass tonight. Me and Shirley had already discussed it, ha! Ha!", me laughing hysterically replying, "Bobby won't be!", me reassuring Meia that I had the situation under control, before I hung up with her.

CHAPTER 10

Never Mess With Family

However, after hanging up with Meia, I came out of Shirleys' bathroom, and Shirley replies to me, "Bobby called, but I didn't pick up the phone. What is his problem? He has a woman. I don't know why I even wasted my time with him, because Bobby was a five minute fuck, by the time Bobby gets finished sucking my breasts, he's ready to pop his cork". I then replied, "What? I think that's too much information". Shirley replies, "No! I want you to know everything". Shirley replies again saying, "A woman doesn't enjoy sex by herself. I'd have to masterbate right in front of him, fuck that and fuck him". So after Shirley explained to me all about Bobbys' personal business, I wanted to bust out laughing hysterically, but I somehow held it in, then Shirley replies, "I am just really going to ignore Bobbys' calls from now on!". Shirley replies again, "I was thinking about the whole relationship. It's no fun being a woman and to have a man, and I still have to fuck myself". I was on the verge of falling off the couch in laughter. Shirley replies again, "He's a computer wizard. It should compute in Bobbys' mind that if I am not calling him back, that he's a computerized sorry dick mother fucker". I then replied to Shirley, "Don't be so uptight. Let's just change the subject". However, I could see that Shirley was frustrated and uptight, and she needed to bust a nut, so I started kissing Shirleys' neck. Remember Shirley had orange looking teeth. I never kissed her in the mouth. It would always be on her neck or cheek bone. However, me and Shirley adjourned to her bedroom. Shirley became an instant freak. Shirley proceeded to put her tongue on my asshole. I replied, "God damn! Hold up, wait a minute! What are you doing?", Shirley replies, "you never had a woman do that to you before?". I replied, "Hell no! But it feels good". I started thinking to myself, this explains the orange teeth, Shirley licking too much ass. I was ready to bust out in laughter again, but it felt really good. I started thinking to myself, "wow", for a school teacher, she does wonders to a head. So after sex, Shirley wanted me to spend the night. At first I was thinking, "hell ya!", but then I thought about it. I had my wallet in my pocket. Every man knows that most women wait until a man is asleep, then she goes through his wallet. I then jumped up out of bed, replying to Shirley, "I left my gas oven on at my house", and yelling, "Oh my God!". This was just an excuse, because I didn't want Shirley to find out about my true identity. Remember I am really Meias' brother, the woman that she replied to me, that she hated and called her a bitch. No one talks about my sister that way. This gave me more of a hard on to finish the job. Meias' plan was working to perfection. Shirley then drops me back off at the service station, and before I got out of Shirleys' car, I promised to call her. Now several weeks have passed. Shirley still didn't have a clue about what was going on, but Meia and me still had to be careful, and not blow the plan, keeping it very secret. However, Shirley had bragged to Bobby about a new guy she had met named John, and that's me. Bobby didn't like it. I mentioned that earlier in the book. Shirley also told Bobby, that John was a successful business man and had a lot of materialistic things. Shirley really bragged to Bobby about John having gold rings and jewelry, etc. Now everytime Bobby would call Shirley, she would talk about John. Bobby was highly upset and beside himself, and I knew this because, most of the time when Bobby called, I was with Shirley. Then a lot of times when Bobby tried to call Shirley, he couldn't get through, because me and Shirley would be on the phone for hours at a time sometimes. Then sometimes, because of my schedule and Shirleys' also, we would not see each other until the weekends. Some of those hours, when me and Shirley would be talking on the phone, Shirley would be depressed and needed someone to talk to, because of her job, then me calming her down in a soft voice. Our conversations would end with Shirley masterbating and calling me daddy, then after Shirley would have an orgasm, she would reply, "I can't wait to see you this weekend", then we would just hang up. I was beginning to wonder, this woman is really falling for me, and this whole relationship scenario was just a joke. All of this just to get revenge on Bobby, for wasting my sister Meias' time for five years. That's a long time to be just playing someone. In my own opinion, if you don't want a relationship with someone anymore, just ell them how you feel. Don't just keep leading them on and using a person, and hurting their feelings, that's wrong! However, now the whole family knows that Bobby's a liar and a cheater. I am wondering to myself, when is Meia going to pull the plug on this whole operation, because Meia now knows the truth about Bobby. Now the holidays are here. Meia kept their relationship going and I am still seeing Shirley on a part time basis. Meia invites Bobby to our family's Thanksgiving dinner, so I replied to Meia, "Are you sure you want to do this? Because I can't look at this man with a straight face, nevertheless talk with him, without laughing". Meia replied, "Everything will be alright", then I replied, "If you say so. Everyone knows that I'm a comedian, and sometimes I can't help myself". Meia replied, "It will be alright!". So we are sitting at the dining room table eating, talking, and laughing. I was really laughing at Bobby. Remember Shirley mentioned to Bobby, that John had a lot of jewelry and diamond rings on each hand. I caught Bobby not looking, because he was eating, and I stretched both of my hands out, waving them like a wand. Everyone started laughing and Meia kicked me in the shin underneath the table. The joke was on Bobby, because everyone knew that John was really me. I fell out of the chair laughing. I had to leave the room to get myself together, before I gave up the plan! I really didn't care, because Bobby was a no good son of a bitch. A lot of men would be glad to have a woman like my sister Meia. A woman who could cook, clean, and is very well educated. Most of the time, in her spare time, the only thing my sister Meia did was go to church. Now what man in his right mind, would mess over a woman like this? After she has already accepted you, along with the baggage that was brought into the relationship. This man was crazy! There were a few times that me and Bobby would hang out, and you could just tell that something was wrong. On one occasion, Bobby was driving and his cell phone rang, and it was Shirley. They were in a deep conversation. He was replying to Shirley, "You don't have time for me anymore, because you're spending all your time with John", and Bobby also replies, "I am going to have to fuck John up". I was looking at Bobby with a crazy look, almost laughing, then Bobby misses his turn. I replied to Bobby, "You just missed your turn", and Shirley hears me and replies, "Who is that?". Bobby replies, "Meias' brother", then Shirley replies to Bobby again on the phone, "His voice sounds so familiar". Bobby realizes that he's not paying attention to the road and hangs up with Shirley. However, another two months go by. Meia is still in a relationship with Bobby. I called Meia on the telephone. I replied, "Hey sis, when are we calling it quits, because I can't take Shirley anymore", then I replied, "Guess what? I ran into Shirley inside of Penn Station. I was walking along with some co workers and I heard someone yelling across the floor. I wasn't paying attention to my surroundings. One of my co workers tapped me on the arm replying, some woman over there is calling you by a different name. I looked in shock and awe, I replied to my co workers, oh shit, go along with what name she's calling me. I'll tell you guys about it later. My co workers were laughing at me, replying to me, who's that? Your babies mama, before Shirley walked over to us". Then meia replies, What! You ran into Shirley". I replied, "Yes, I had to lie to my co workers, then having to explain what the situation was about when we returned to work, so while at work sitting at my desk, I am telling the guys and girls about it. I was surprised to hear from the women, their response was, that's good for the bitch, that could have been my husband or boyfriend". Then I replied, "Do you think I am wrong?". The woman in the office replied, "Hell No! That bitch really got what she deserves, especially when she already knew that Bobby had a woman", and most of the guys replied, "he got what was coming to him, because no man would stand by and let someone try to make a fool out of his sister, if they could help it". They also replied, "So how was she in bed?". I replied, "She's a teacher. She gives good head lessons". The whole office erupted in laughter. How could you sleep with a man you don't even know, and furthermore, accept flowers from a stranger you've never seen before! Stop! Ladies, if you call a mans house and a woman answers the phone, you should investigate it, before you sleep with him, or even continue to have a conversation with him. Some guys will lie and say, "That's my good friend from work, or that's my sister". Ladies, go and investigate right away, because if you wait, most of the time it's too late, then you can't change the fate in the relationship. In this story, Shirley didn't care. She listened to Bobbys' wall of lies that my sister was just his friend. I can't imagine how my sister felt, when she asked Shirley to quit calling the house, and the woman Shirley kept disrespecting her, because Bobby communicated to Shirley that he had no woman, and it was safe to call his house, that's all out disrespectful. So everytime me and Shirley would have sex, I would purposely hurt her, by shoving my penis into her very hard, showing my displeasure to her, for what she was doing to Meia. I knew Shirley was a liar, just like Bobby, for the simple fact that Shirley promised not to call or answer Bobbys' phone calls. You can't turn a hoe into a housewife, and furthermore, I had no real feelings for Shirley, because the whole relationship was a sham, just to bust Mr. So Called Mr. Perfect Bobby, to help Meia get her revenge! However, the following week, Meia called me and replied, "I've just taken all of my stuff out of his house and took everything back to my place". Meia replied again, "I had to hurry up before Bobby got off from work. I left him a voice message replying, "Game over player!". I then replied to Meia, "your shitting me, stop pulling my leg, you really did that!". Meia replies, "Now you can stop seeing Shirley". I then replied, "Great!". I immediately had my second cell phone turned off and didn't contact Shirley anymore, so now Meia isn't speaking to Bobby anymore. Bobby kept calling her at work and at home. Meia wasn't returning his phone calls. Meia replies to me, "I wish Bobby would stop calling me. When I was living with him, I didn't get this much respect. Why now all of a sudden? Bobby was telling women that he didn't have a woman, and I was either his sister or some co worker friend from work. The hell with him! There are other fish in the sea. No woman should put up with being second rate to another woman. I did a lot for him, how dare him to treat me this way. I am totally done with him". So now Bobby is mad and beside himself. Bobby is now trying to reach Meia by emails, leaving her nasty messages. He's mad, because Meia is not talking to him. However, I told Meia, "Bobby is now calling me everyday, trying to get me to plead his case to you". Meia replies, "I don't have anything to say to him, but you can still talk to him, if you want to. I don't mind if you still want to remain friends with him". I then replied to Meia, "You've got to be kidding me", laughing hysterically, I then replied, "I fucked his mistress. Now he has no one to blame but himself. Now I am feeling really bad, because he's trying to cry on my shoulder, after you paid for everything, for me to fuck his mistress". Meia replies, "This should teach men a lesson, that a woman is always smarter than a man, because when a man sleeps, a woman is always thinking. Bobby should have thought about that before he cheated on me, and then replying to Shirley that I was his friend from work. I don't give a flying fuck if he uses his hand every night. He has Vaseline lotion on his dresser. No man is ever going to cheat on me again and get away with it. So many men are doing this today and there getting away with it. Some get caught and some don't, but Bobby got caught red handed with his pants down". Meia replies again, "I'll be a fool to go back to him. Once a cheater, always a cheater. If I were you, I wouldn't feel sorry for him. Didn't you have fun screwing Shirley?". I then replied to Meia, "Hell yah! Shirley was definitely a freak. Shirley used her tongue like toilet paper, but when I first saw Shirley, I wanted to run back out of the hospital room. Her hair really looked like chicken scratch". I replied again saying, "I did it for you sis. I did it for love". I then grabbed my sister Meia and hugged her, also replying, telling her, "God will send you a good man, just hold on. He'll fix it". However, my mother use to tell us, there's a price to pay for the wrongs that you do in life. There is a thing called karma, always treat people like you want to be treated. We as men need to check ourselves, and stop putting the blame on someone else, if your wrong, your wrong. Quit making excuses for your actions and deal with the consequences and remember, one mans loss, is another mans gain. However, Meia didn't lose any sleep over the breakup. She kept going on like nothing had ever happened. At first Meia seemed upset and very sad, but she faced reality, the relationship was over and life goes on. However, Meia finally met another man. This guy was nice. He was also a church going man, that was right up Meias' alley. A friend of Meias' from work introduced them to one another. The friend from work thought that they would make a perfect couple. Ladies and gentlemen, please remember, all players generally end up by themselves, However, we as men never think that we can be caught, but temptation is the multitude of all evil. Ladies, it's true, almost all men use the power of lies to get the pussy. Men have been enslaved since the beginning of time, when Eve persuaded Adam to take a bite from the forbidden fruit, that's in the Bible. However, the bottom line is, both women and men should never be tempted, if there in a marriage or in a serious relationship. Guess what? My sister Meia is set to be married soon, after wasting precious time with someone who really didn't care about her. If you love someone, MEN!, don't cheat on your wives or girlfriends. The bottom line is, sooner or later you will get caught. There's nothing worth risking the love of your life. Stay true to the man or woman that you love, and remember, players almost always get played in the end, because in my own opinion, a woman is always smarter, because she thinks while a man is sleep, always being one step ahead of the game. MEN!, remember payback is a bitch, so stay true and practice what you preach! LADIES!, remember if a man doesn't respect you enough to wear his wedding ring get rid of him, chances are he's cheating on you. However, some men and women do this sending signals that they are available. If your mate doesn't respect a symbol of love, chances are their not respecting you. LADIES!, please stop believing everything a man tells you. The biggest excuse a man uses is, "Honey I am working late at the office". The bottom line is Ladies and Gentlemen, never assume that the truth is being told all the time. Please investigate your mate!

THE END

www.ingramcontent.com/pod-product-compliance
Lightning Source LLC
Chambersburg PA
CBHW021248280526
45784CB00005B/2290